A HAITIAN FAMILY

A HAITIAN FAMILY

By Keith Elliot Greenberg

Lerner Publications Company ◆ Minneapolis

This book is available in two editions:
Library binding by Lerner Publications Company
Soft cover by First Avenue Editions
241 First Avenue North
Minneapolis, MN 55401
ISBN: 0–8225–3410–X (lib. bdg. : alk. paper)
ISBN: 0–8225–9776–4 (pbk.)

A pronunciation guide can be found on page 54.
The interviews for this book were conducted in late 1995 and in 1996.

LIBRARY OF CONGRESS CATALOGING-IN-PUBLICATION DATA

Greenberg, Keith Elliot.
   A Haitian Family / Keith Elliot Greenberg.
    p. cm. — (Journey between two worlds)
   Includes bibliographical references and index.
   Summary: Chronicles the history of Haiti and the efforts of one Haitian family to emigrate to the United States and rebuild their lives in Brooklyn, N.Y.
   ISBN 0–8225–3410–X (lib. bdg. : alk. paper)
   1. Haitian American families—New York (State)—New York—Juvenile literature. 2. Haitian Americans—New York (State)—New York—Juvenile literature. 3. Refugees, Political—New York (State)—New York—Juvenile literature. 4. Refugees, Political—Haiti—Juvenile literature. 5. Brooklyn (New York, N.Y.)—Social life and customs—Juvenile literature. 6. New York (N.Y.)—Social life and customs—Juvenile literature. 7. Civil rights—Haiti—Juvenile literature. 8. Haiti—Emigration and immigration—Juvenile literature. [1. Haitian Americans. 2. Refugees. 3. Haiti—History.] I. Title. II. Series
   F129.B7G695   1998
   974.7′10049697294—dc20   96–17183

Manufactured in the United States of America
1 2 3 4 5 6 – SP – 03 02 01 00 99 98

AUTHOR'S NOTE

The author wishes to extend his thanks for the assistance and hospitality of the Beaubrun family, of Father Sam Sansaricq of St. Jerome's Church, and of the staff of *Haiti Progress* newspaper. Special thanks to Kim Ives, who generously shared his skills in translating Creole to English and back again.

For decades Haiti's military police (above) *attacked those who spoke out against the government. In addition to political violence, Haiti's people had economic concerns as well. Slums* (facing page) *are still common in the cities of Haiti, the poorest nation in the Western Hemisphere.*

SERIES INTRODUCTION

What they have left behind is sometimes a living nightmare of war and hunger that most Americans can hardly begin to imagine. As refugees set out to start a new life in another country, they are torn by many feelings. They may wish they didn't have to leave their homeland. They may fear giving up the only life they have ever known. Many may also feel excitement and hope as they struggle to build a better life in a new country.

People who move from one place to another are called migrants. Two types of migrants are immigrants and refugees. Immigrants choose to leave their homelands, usually to improve their standards of living. They may be leaving behind poverty, famine (hunger), or a failing economy. They may be pursuing a better job or reuniting with family members.

Refugees, on the other hand, often have no choice but to flee their homeland to protect their own personal safety. How could anyone be in so much danger?

The Beaubrun family were among thousands who fled Haiti's military dictatorship in the early 1990s. Natalie (right) was just a baby when the family left Haiti.

The government of his or her country is either unable or unwilling to protect its citizens from persecution, or cruel treatment. In many cases, the government is actually the cause of the persecution. Government leaders or another group within the country may be persecuting anyone of a certain race, religion, or ethnic background. Or they may persecute those who belong to a particular social group or who hold political opinions that are not accepted by the government.

From the 1950s through the mid-1970s, the number of refugees worldwide held steady at between 1.5 and 2.5 million. The number began to rise sharply in 1976. By the mid-1990s, it approached 20 million. These figures do not include people who are fleeing disasters such as famine (estimated to be at least 10 million). Nor do they include those who are forced to leave their homes but stay within their own countries (about 27 million).

As this rise in refugees and other migrants continues, countries that have long welcomed newcomers are beginning to close their doors. Some U.S. citizens question whether the United States should accept refugees when it cannot even meet the needs of all its own people. On the other hand, experts point out that the number of refugees is small—less than 20 percent of all migrants worldwide—so refugees really don't have a very big impact on the nation. Still others suggest that the tide of refugees could be slowed through greater efforts to address the problems that force people to flee. There are no easy answers in this ongoing debate.

This book is one in a series called *Journey Between Two Worlds,* which looks at the lives of refugee families—their difficulties and triumphs. Each book describes the journey of a family from their homeland to the United States and how they adjust to a new life in America while still preserving traditions from their homeland. The series makes no attempt to join the debate about refugees. Instead, *Journey Between Two Worlds* hopes to give readers a better understanding of the daily struggles and joys of a refugee family.

Many of the refugees who fled Haiti were intercepted by the U.S. Coast Guard and held in camps at Guantánamo Bay, Cuba.

 When nine-year-old Gregory Beaubrun thinks about Haiti—the country where he was born—he remembers the good things. In his hometown of Port-au-Prince, the weather was warm all year long. Every Sunday he and his family dressed up and went to church together. There were always lots of kids around to play soccer. Children would laugh as they watched men play dominoes on the street—especially when the losers had to stick clothespins to their faces.

But there is another side to Haiti. When many Americans think of this island nation in the Caribbean Sea, they imagine a tense country. For much of the 1900s, Haiti was ruled by harsh military dictators. Newspapers and radio stations that criticized the government were closed down. Soldiers battled demonstrators in the streets. People who demanded freedom or spoke out against the government were taken from their homes and thrown in jail. Many were tortured and killed. As a result of this political violence, many Haitians have fled to the United States over the years.

Young people play soccer in front of the National Palace in Port-au-Prince, Haiti, the Beaubruns' hometown. Being victims of police brutality like this man (below) led the family to flee the country.

In 1991 the military overthrew Haiti's first democratically elected president, Jean-Bertrand Aristide. Thousands of Haitians again fled the violence in their country. They piled onto small boats, risking their lives crossing the rough seawaters that separate Haiti from the United States, where the refugees hoped to make a better life.

So much has happened to Gregory and his father, Bazelais, his mother, Doudoune, and his younger sister, Natalie. In the early 1990s, his father's life was threatened for speaking out against the violence of Haiti's military government. Gregory's mother was beaten up by military men in uniform.

Fearing for their lives, the family finally escaped Haiti in 1992. Along with 300 other Haitian refugees, the Beaubruns jammed onto a flimsy boat headed for the United States. Along the way, the U.S. Coast Guard—which patrolled the waters to look for fleeing Haitians—stopped the small vessel. But instead of

Guarded by the U.S. military, the Haitian refugees at Guantánamo Bay had to wait for months to see whether they would be granted freedom to come to the United States or be forced to return to Haiti, where they would face more danger.

bringing the group to America, the Coast Guard took the refugees to a special camp for Haitian "boat people"—a term referring to the thousands of people fleeing Haiti by boat.

The camp was located at the U.S. naval base at Guantánamo Bay, located on the southeastern coast of the nearby island of Cuba. The camp was hot and dirty. All the refugees there worried about being sent back to Haiti, where they feared they would be punished by the very people they were fleeing. This had already happened to many of the Haitian boat people. At the camp, U.S. officials interviewed the Haitians and sent back those who could not prove they were political refugees (people whose lives are at risk in their home- lands because of their political beliefs). Back in Haiti, some of the returning refugees were instantly arrested. Others immediately went into hiding. Some of the re- turning boat people were killed.

At Guantanamo Bay, U.S. immigration officials in- terviewed Gregory's parents. Bazelais made it very clear that he had been an outspoken opponent of Haiti's military government. He told the officials that if he had not fled Haiti, he would have been killed. After three long months, the immigration officials decided that Gregory's parents qualified as political refugees. They gave the family permission to resettle in the United States.

Life at the refugee camp was often hot and boring.

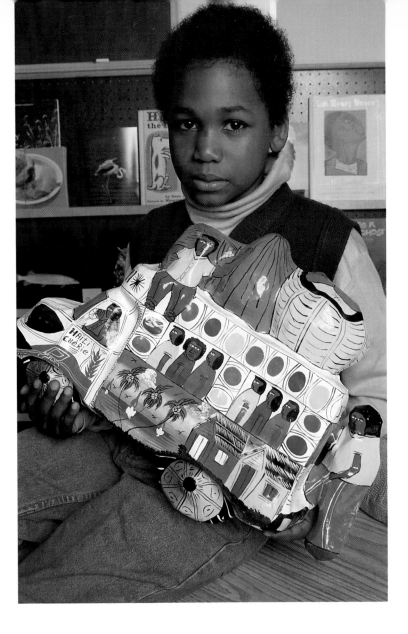

Gregory's colorful papier-mâché bus, with the words Haïti Chérie *(or "Dearest Haiti") printed on the front, reminds him of his Caribbean homeland.*

Gregory has a new life in Flatbush—a largely Haitian neighborhood in Brooklyn, New York. He lives in a small apartment with his parents, his sister, Natalie (6), and two brothers, Steve (2) and infant Kelly, both born in the United States.

Of the 1.5 million Haitians in North America, about 500,000 live in the New York area. It is difficult to know the exact number, because many Haitians come to the United States illegally and live and work in secret. Other cities with large numbers of Haitians are Miami, which is in Florida, and Montreal, in the Canadian province of Quebec.

Bazelais, Gregory's father, works as a cook in a candy factory. Gregory's mother earns money babysitting for neighbors' children. When Bazelais has time off, he and Gregory take the subway to Prospect Park, the largest park in Brooklyn. They take a soccer ball with them to kick back and forth.

Gregory likes playing hide-and-seek in the family's apartment and attending fourth grade at Public School 6 (or, P.S. 6)—a neighborhood school. His favorite television show is *The Fresh Prince of Bel-Air*. His favorite basketball player is Shaquille O'Neal.

Gregory speaks English better than anyone in his family. The others are more comfortable speaking Creole, one of Haiti's two official languages. Creole is a combination of French (Haiti's other official language) and the many African languages spoken by the slaves who were brought to Haiti hundreds of years ago.

"I know I'm different than other kids because I wasn't born in America," Gregory says. "I have different customs and speak a different language. But I'm just a regular kid."

Gregory (center), *his sister, Natalie* (left), *and their cousin Stefanie* (right) *play on the swing set near their apartment building in Brooklyn, New York.*

Haiti is a mountainous country in the West Indies—a group of tropical islands that lie between the southeastern United States and the northern coast of South America. Haiti takes up the western third of an island called Hispaniola. Another country, the Dominican Republic, lies on the eastern side of the island.

On a map, Haiti is shaped something like a horseshoe. In between the northern and southern arms of the horseshoe lies the Gulf of Gonâve. Off the gulf coast lie two smaller islands, Gonâve and Grande Cayemite. The Gulf of Gonâve is an arm of the Caribbean Sea, which laps against the nation's southern shores. To Haiti's north is the Atlantic Ocean. The Windward

Haiti's coastline and mountains are picturesque. In the early 1990s, the sea was a means of escape from Haiti.

17

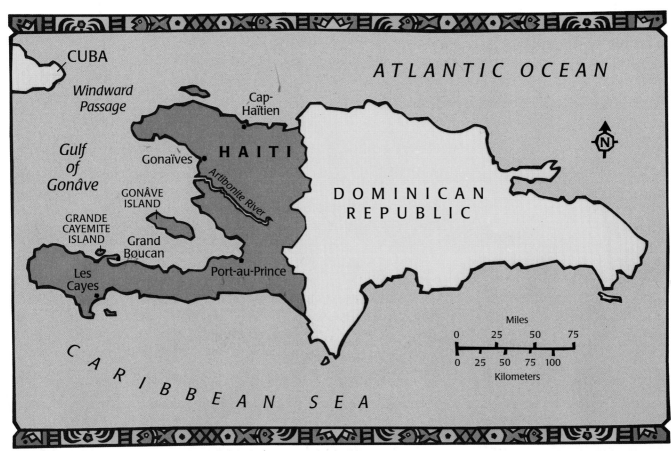

Haiti occupies about one-third of the island of Hispaniola in the Caribbean Sea. Haiti shares its eastern border with the Dominican Republic.

Passage separates Haiti from the island nation of Cuba to the northwest.

Black people make up about 95 percent of Haiti's population. Most are descended from West Africans, who were brought to Haiti as slaves starting in the 1500s. The remaining 5 percent of the population are mulattoes (Haitians with both black ancestors and white ancestors). Only about one-third of Haiti's people reside in cities. The rest live in rural areas, where they farm small plots of land. In the mountains, people grow coffee and cacao, from which cocoa and chocolate are made. Popular tropical fruits include limes, guavas, and mangoes. Farmers in the Artibonite River valley in eastern Haiti raise rice and sugarcane.

Small plots on steeply sloped terrain (below left) provide food for Haitians in highland communities. Rice (below), which is raised in the Artibonite River valley, is a staple of the Haitian diet.

Selling sugar and coffee to foreign countries earns money for Haiti. But Haiti's farmers can't depend on a good selling price for these crops because the price changes frequently—up one day and down the next. The country has few industries, and many Haitians are unemployed. In fact, Haiti is the poorest nation in the Western Hemisphere.

Haiti does have some valuable minerals, such as gold and copper, but not enough to attract mining companies. Hundreds of years ago, these minerals attracted Europeans to what is now Haiti. Christopher Columbus, an explorer working for Spain, landed on the island in 1492. After he found gold in the eastern part of Hispaniola, Spanish settlers came to the island. They forced the indigenous (native, or Indian) peoples to work as slaves and dig for the precious metal. In less than 20 years, most of the Indians were wiped out by overwork, deadly European diseases, and fighting with other regional Indian groups. The Spanish then began forcibly transporting Africans to the island to replace the Indian slaves.

Meanwhile, the French were settling coastal areas of western Hispaniola. By 1697 Spain had turned over control of the western part of the island to France, which named its new colony (overseas settlement) Saint-Domingue. Like the Spanish before them, the French brought slaves from Africa to the island. The

In 1492 Christopher Columbus became the first European explorer to set foot on the island of Hispaniola.

Spanish conquerors forced the native population of the island of Hispaniola to search for gold.

slaves worked on coffee and spice plantations (large farms). This system of forced labor allowed France to turn Saint-Domingue into one of its richest colonies.

The slaves in Saint-Domingue suffered discrimination and abuse. The French did not allow slaves to own land or to vote. *Gens de couleur* (mulattoes and other people of mixed racial heritage) had more rights than slaves but were not allowed to hold certain jobs, run for government office, or marry whites. By the late 1700s, both slaves and gens de couleur were ready to fight for their freedom.

A slave rebellion in Saint-Domingue in 1791 started a revolution that lasted 13 years. By 1800 Toussaint

Louverture, one of the leaders of the revolution, had gained control of the entire island and abolished slavery. However, Toussaint never officially declared the island to be independent from France. In 1802 the French sent troops to topple Toussaint and to reestablish full control of the colony. Toussaint was captured and sent to France, where he died in prison in 1803.

But the revolution could not be stopped. General Jean-Jacques Dessalines, a former slave, became the new leader of the revolution. In 1804 he declared independence for the western half of the island and named himself emperor of the new nation. Haiti was the first independent black country in the Western Hemisphere.

After a 13-year revolution, Haiti won its independence from France in 1804.

In 1844 the eastern part of Hispaniola declared its independence as a free and separate nation called the Dominican Republic. Meanwhile, Haiti's governments changed quickly and violently.

The United States looked on nervously. U.S. bankers and businesspeople worried about losing the money they had invested in Haiti. And during World War I (1914–1918), the United States feared that Germany—an enemy nation—was gaining too much influence in Haiti. To restore order, to protect U.S. money, and to make sure that other countries didn't take over Haiti during wartime, the U.S. Marines invaded Haiti in 1915.

During the U.S. occupation, some things in Haiti improved. For example, schools, hospitals, and highways were built. But many Haitians hated the idea of a foreign power running their country. As U.S. companies began buying plantations and building factories in Haiti, Haitian rebels attacked marines and other U.S. targets. U.S. troops finally left Haiti in 1934.

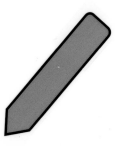

The infamous Tontons Macoutes—the brutal secret-police force established by Haitian president François Duvalier—patrolled Haiti's streets and instilled fear in the people.

In 1957, after a series of military officers had ruled Haiti, a doctor named François Duvalier was elected president. He had a good reputation in the country and was given the nickname "Papa Doc." As time passed, Duvalier turned into a vicious dictator. In 1964 he announced that he was president for life. He outlawed political parties and shut down newspapers that opposed him. It became a crime to criticize the government. People who did were arrested and jailed without a trial. Prisoners were tortured and killed.

When Haitians protested for more liberty or tried to overthrow Duvalier, they were attacked by the Tontons Macoutes—Duvalier's brutal secret police. During Duvalier's 14-year presidency, the Macoutes are believed to have killed at least 20,000 fellow Haitians.

Before Duvalier died in 1971, he named his son, Jean-Claude, to replace him. The younger Duvalier—called "Baby Doc"—was only 19 years old. Like his father, he used arrests, torture, and the Tontons Macoutes to overpower his opponents.

By the 1980s, years of political corruption and misuse of government money had left Haiti one of the poorest countries in the world. The average Haitian made less than $400 a year. Half the population could not read. Malaria and other tropical diseases were common. People also suffered from illnesses caused by poor sanitation. Many Haitians didn't have enough food and were on the verge of starvation. With poverty everywhere, Haiti's environment suffered too. Trees were chopped down for fuel and cropland until the country's forests were almost completely destroyed.

Beginning in the mid-1980s, large groups of Haitians began to protest against Baby Doc and the years of oppression and corruption of the Duvalier family. In 1986 Duvalier fled to France, fearing that he would be killed if he remained in Haiti.

Although dictators continued to govern the country, Haitians were always searching for change. Jean-Bertrand Aristide was a Roman Catholic priest who was not afraid to criticize his country's leaders. In emotional sermons, he preached against corrupt politicians, businesspeople, and leaders of his own church—anyone he believed was harming Haiti. The country's military rulers considered Aristide a dangerous man. There were at least four attempts to kill him. But no one could take away his popularity. Around Haiti he became known as *ti pwofet* ("little prophet") and *Msieu Mirak* ("Mr. Miracle").

Jean-Claude Duvalier, or "Baby Doc," succeeded his father as Haiti's leader. He maintained an oppressive grip on the population as his father had before him.

In 1988 opponents of Jean-Bertrand Aristide (facing page, inset) *burned the church* (facing page) *where he preached. By 1990 Haitians were celebrating Aristide's victory* (right) *in Haiti's first fair, democratic presidential elections.*

In 1990 Aristide ran for president, promising reform. His political movement was called *Lavalas* ("flash flood") because people compared it to a sudden and cleansing downpour. In December 1990, Aristide was elected president of Haiti in the nation's first democratic elections. As president, Aristide promised to lift Haiti out of poverty and to bring the Tontons Macoutes to justice. Many people believed that under Aristide, Haiti would finally experience democracy.

But before these dreams could be realized, the military overthrew Aristide in 1991, forcing the president out of Haiti. His supporters found themselves in constant danger of kidnapping, torture, and death at the hands of the Macoutes and the military. People like Gregory's father—a loyal Aristide supporter—feared they would be murdered if they stayed in Haiti.

Bazelais steals a tranquil moment to reflect on a past filled with fear, frustration, and finally, hope for a better life for his family.

 When Bazelais Beaubrun isn't busy working or helping his wife take care of their children, he sits quietly and remembers the relatives and friends he cared about in Haiti. Some of them managed to escape to the United States. But many died, simply because they wanted their government to treat them fairly.

"When a Haitian person talks about brothers and sisters, the meaning is different than in America," Bazelais says. "To a Haitian, brothers and sisters can also be cousins or even very good friends. Today so many people I called my brothers and sisters are dead. I'm a young man. But I've suffered so much tragedy."

Bazelais never wanted special privileges from his government. All he wanted was equal treatment. He was born in 1965 and grew up in the small town of Grand Boucan in southern Haiti. There were few jobs there, so Bazelais traveled to Port-au-Prince to find work. There he got a job operating a *borlette,* a small stand for selling lottery tickets. He also met Doudoune in Haiti's capital. They married in 1987, one year after Gregory was born.

Doudoune is from a Port-au-Prince neighborhood called Carrefours Feuilles, which means "Crossroads of Leaves." It's a dirty, crowded place, where many of the streets aren't paved. When it rains, the roads turn to mud. Over the years, many poor people from Haiti's rural areas have moved to this neighborhood to live while searching for work in the city.

When Gregory was a baby, his grandmother took care of him while Doudoune and Bazelais were at work. Doudoune earned money selling soaps and shampoos in the neighborhood marketplace. At the end of the day, Doudoune would take her son back to

In Haiti Bazelais worked in a borlette *selling lottery tickets.*

the couple's apartment, which was located in a group of small homes set close together. Bazelais' mother, brother, and sister lived there, too.

Bazelais insists he never looked for trouble. But if he saw something he considered unjust, he spoke out about it. Aristide's election in 1990 raised the couple's hopes. Bazelais and Doudoune believed that, with a just leader in Haiti, their children would be able to grow up in peace.

Haitians line up (above) in 1990 to participate in Haiti's first peaceful, democratic elections. Graffiti (right) in Port-au-Prince supported Aristide's campaign for president. In this painting, the rooster symbolizing Aristide's Lavalas movement steps on the neck of a guinea hen—the symbol of the Duvaliers. The number five signifies the ranking of Aristide's party on the ballot.

But when the military overthrew Aristide the next year, Bazelais could sense that danger was near. Members of the Tontons Macoutes came around to the family's neighborhood, beating up people who supported democracy in Haiti. Still Bazelais did not keep quiet. He told everybody who would listen that the Macoutes were wrong and that people in Haiti should band together and demand liberty. Occasionally he learned about community meetings organized by people who wanted to restore democracy to Haiti. Whenever he could, Bazelais attended.

Some members of the Tontons Macoutes told Bazelais that they knew how to shut him up. One day when he wouldn't expect it, they said, they would shoot him. Bazelais argued that he was doing nothing wrong. In the future, he promised, Haiti would be free of the Tontons Macoutes and other criminals.

The Macoutes did everything possible to terrify Bazelais. One day they beat up Doudoune in the street. As they hit her, they dared Bazelais to strike them. But he could only stand by and watch. He knew that if he got involved, they would claim that he had attacked them. They would kill Bazelais and Doudoune, saying that the two had started the fight. Then the couple's children would grow up as orphans.

One night as Bazelais was returning home from work, some neighbors stopped him. They pointed to

Bazelais and Doudoune wanted democracy in their homeland so their kids could go to school and live in a peaceful nation.

two strange cars parked in front of the house. They warned Bazelais, "Don't go in. They're going to kill you."

Soldiers were going from house to house, hoping to catch Aristide supporters. Soldiers had already come into the Beaubruns' home and beaten Doudoune again. Bazelais' brother was placed under arrest. He was dragged out of the house and never seen or heard from again.

The family knew that the soldiers planned to do the same thing to Bazelais and urged him to run. So Bazelais fled to another part of Port-au-Prince. Then he took a boat on the Gulf of Gonâve to his hometown. He thought he'd be safe there, but he was wrong.

After overthrowing Aristide, Haiti's military government demanded that people listen only to news on radio stations run by the Haitian government. Bazelais

After Aristide's overthrow in 1991, many Haitians prayed for the terror to end and for Aristide to be returned to the presidency.

Demonstrators in Miami, Florida, protested Aristide's overthrow by flying Haitian flags and displaying wooden roosters—the symbol of Aristide's Lavalas movement.

knew that the broadcasters on these stations were telling only the military's side of things. So one night, Bazelais gathered with some men in a yard to listen to the Voice of America, a radio station run by the U.S. government. Suddenly a Macoute came by and began threatening the group. The men scattered as the Macoute fired two shots into the air.

Bazelais knew that he would be arrested or killed if he remained in town. For safety he had to keep moving. Between 100,000 and 300,000 Haitians found

Gregory was afraid of the ride. "I worried we'd be eaten by sharks," he says. He and Natalie cried for much of the trip across the rough sea. Because there were so many people squeezed close together in the small, open boat, it was hard to lie down and go to sleep. But even at the worst moments, Bazelais and Doudoune told their children, "Don't worry. Everything will be okay. Soon we'll be safe."

Meanwhile, many U.S. citizens were complaining about the large number of Haitians heading to Florida, the state closest to Haiti. Some Americans feared the newcomers would take jobs away from them. Others were concerned about the money the U.S. government would spend to support the refugees, many of whom were poor and uneducated.

To calm the outcry, the U.S. Coast Guard stationed ships along the route between Haiti and Florida. The Coast Guard stopped Haitian vessels and took the boat people to Guantánamo Bay.

After several days at sea, Gregory and his family were taken to the camp at Guantánamo Bay. Although they wished they had made it all the way to the United States, they also felt relieved. At least at Guantánamo Bay they would be safe from the Tontons Macoutes.

Gregory had another reason to be grateful. "Our boat kept rocking," he says. "I thought we were going to sink in the ocean."

A detail from a painting by a Haitian refugee at Guantánamo Bay (facing page) *shows Haitian refugees being rescued at sea by a U.S. helicopter. The Beaubruns' boat was intercepted at sea. The passengers were brought to Guantánamo Bay* (above), *where refugees sweltered in tents on the hot concrete.*

The three months the family spent at Guantánamo Bay seemed much longer. Unmarried men were housed in one section of the camp, unmarried women in another. Gregory and his parents stayed in a tent set up on a scorching hot airplane runway. They ate tuna casserole and other prepackaged meals they weren't used to. The family didn't care for these foods, but there was nothing else to eat.

The days were hot and dusty. It was hard to find a shady spot because very few trees grew at the camp. Lizards and bugs were everywhere. So were long, groundhog-sized rodents that everyone called "banana rats."

The U.S. Navy had put up a few basketball hoops, and there were a couple places to play soccer. But mainly people just waited around. Gregory was bored because there wasn't a school for the refugee children.

"I asked my father all the time when they were going to let us go to America," Gregory recalls.

Bazelais would answer, "Don't worry. We'll get there." But he was growing frustrated himself. It seemed as if he were in jail. He had to eat whatever he was served. And though he had relatives in other parts of the camp, he was forbidden to visit them. The Beaubruns felt as if they were being punished just because they wanted to live in a free country.

Life for Haitian refugees at Guantánamo Bay meant lots of waiting. Long lines (top) *formed at mealtimes. And with nowhere to run and play, children* (right) *were very bored.*

With each passing month, the United States grew more and more reluctant to allow the Haitian refugees into the country. Some Americans claimed that the Haitians were lying when they said their lives were in danger. The refugees were accused of trying to enter the United States only because they could make more money there.

Haitians and their supporters were insulted by these types of charges. They noted that people from places like Russia and Ireland seemed to have an easier time being admitted into the United States. It seemed natural to wonder if Haitians were being kept out because they were black.

U.S. officials finally interviewed Gregory's father. They asked him if he wanted to go back to Haiti. Bazelais couldn't believe his ears. "Do you know what would happen to me if you sent me home?" he exclaimed. "If I return to Haiti, I'm a dead man."

Eventually Bazelais was allowed to meet with U.S. immigration officials. For four hours, he described his situation—the threats he had received, his wife's beatings, his brother's disappearance, his concerns about his children's safety. When the discussion was over, there was no question that Bazelais and his family deserved to immigrate to the United States.

The Beaubruns were among the lucky ones. Only one-quarter of the Haitians at Guantánamo Bay were granted the right to come to the United States. The rest either remained at the camp or were returned to Haiti, with all its poverty and violence.

 Most of the Haitian refugees wanted to go to Miami, Florida, which has a very large Haitian community. Gregory's family was different. They had relatives who had fled earlier to Brooklyn, New York. So when the Beaubruns were allowed to leave Guantánamo Bay, they went to New York.

Many Haitian immigrants stay with relatives when they first arrive in the United States. Relying on family is part of the Haitian tradition. For example, when people from Haiti's countryside move to Port-au-Prince, they knock on relatives' doors. People open their homes to cousins they have never met before. They share food and help their relatives find jobs.

The Beaubruns are part of New York City's large Haitian population of approximately 500,000 people.

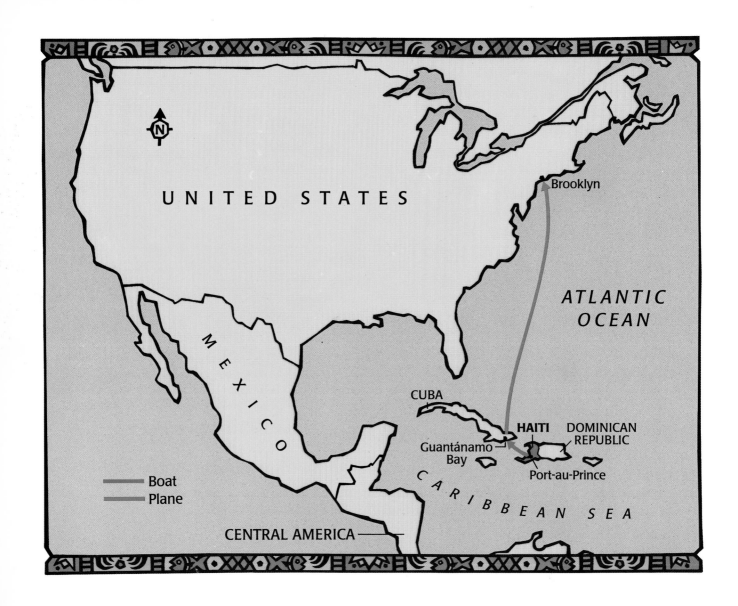

In Brooklyn three different Haitian families may share one apartment. While the children go to school, the men find jobs as factory workers, cab drivers, security guards, and office cleaners. Many of the women get work caring for the elderly or for small children. Much of the money families earn is sent to poorer relatives in Haiti.

Bazelais' brother Tess already had a job in a candy factory in Brooklyn. Then, shortly after Bazelais and his family arrived in New York, Tess was hit by a car and died. Bazelais was given his brother's job at the factory.

Tess's death shocked Bazelais. It seemed so unfair that a man who had survived the violence in Haiti would die crossing the street in New York.

Although many immigrants say their dream is to come to the United States, Bazelais has seen some things he doesn't like about the country. Soon after moving to Brooklyn, he witnessed a shooting in the street. While people in Haiti are killed because of their political beliefs, New York murders frequently involve drugs and money. Either way Bazelais and Doudoune worry about their children.

The Beaubruns live in a neighborhood of aging apartment buildings. Many hardworking families live in the area, but drug dealers are also in the neighborhood. They stand openly on certain blocks, carrying

Gang graffiti covers many buildings in the Beaubruns' neighborhood in Brooklyn. A map (facing page) *shows the route the family took before finally landing in their new home.*

guns and bullying people. For safety Bazelais and Doudoune allow their children to play only in the apartment or in the hallway with other kids. Gregory and his sister and brothers are not allowed outside the building unless an adult is watching them. Newspapers in New York are full of stories about kids who have wandered into the middle of gunfights. Gregory's parents don't want this to happen to their children.

 There are many things about Brooklyn the Beaubruns enjoy. Haitians in the family's neighborhood gather at St. Joseph's Barber Shop. The store is decorated with Haitian flags and pictures of the country's heroes. It doesn't matter whether a visitor wants a haircut or not. People come to the shop to discuss Haitian politics, immigration laws, and local gossip. A minister even conducts Bible-study class in the basement.

Every September New Yorkers from Caribbean countries such as Trinidad, Jamaica, and Haiti line up on Brooklyn's Eastern Parkway to watch the Caribbean Day (or, West Indian Day) Parade. It's one of New York City's biggest festivals. Steel bands play music on the backs of trucks, dancers perform in wild, colorful costumes, and vendors sell food prepared on

A Caribbean immigrant sells grilled ears of corn on the street during Brooklyn's Caribbean Day.

sidewalk barbecues. The Caribbean Day Parade is a version of the Mardi Gras celebration. Mardi Gras takes place in February or March, just before the beginning of Lent, a period of fasting before Easter. But because the weather is still cold and snowy in New York at this time of year, people wait until the end of summer to celebrate.

There are also celebrations for special Haitian holidays. Gédé, for example, is similar to Halloween but is celebrated on November 1 and 2. In New York, as in Haiti, Haitians go to the cemetery to honor the spirits of their ancestors by lighting candles and making offerings, such as rum, food, and money, to the dead. On October 17, Haitian New Yorkers mark Jean-Jacques Dessalines Day, a holiday devoted to the champion of the Haitian revolution. Dessalines' story is taught in Brooklyn schools that have large numbers of Haitian students.

Revelers wear bright, flashy attire during the Caribbean Day Parade (above). *People offer money and light candles in memory of loved ones* (left) *on Gédé in a Port-au-Prince cemetery.*

Some Haitian New Yorkers celebrate Columbus Day on December 5—the day Columbus is said to have landed in Haiti. But many Haitians don't celebrate this day. They hold Columbus and the Europeans who came after him responsible for destroying Haiti's land, killing Indian peoples, and enslaving Africans.

In Haiti Gregory used to eat sugarcane as a treat. In Brooklyn he eats American-style hot dogs instead, along with the candy his father brings home from the factory. But Gregory still likes Haitian meals, especially conch (a shellfish), rice and beans, and chicken with a special seasoning called Creole sauce.

Like most Haitians, the Beaubruns are Catholic. In New York, Gregory and his family attend St. Jerome's Church. A Haitian priest, Father Sam Sansaricq, preaches to his congregation in Creole.

Some Haitians in Brooklyn also practice voodoo, a religion whose followers worship their ancestors and a number of different gods. When slaves were brought to Haiti from West Africa, they brought their voodoo beliefs with them. Although many slaves converted to Christianity, they continued to practice voodoo as well. Over time some Christian symbols and prayers were mixed in with voodoo traditions. Nowadays people who practice voodoo pray for the same things as followers of other religions—good health, success, and happiness.

Doudoune prepares crab, Creole-style, on a hot summer day.

A group of Haitians gather for a voodoo ceremony. Voodoo is a widely practiced religion in Haiti.

 Gregory's little brother Steve has long hair. When some people first see Steve, they think he's a girl. Parents in Haiti don't cut a son's hair until the child is four years old. Bazelais explains that Haitians have a saying that if the hair is trimmed earlier, the child will lose his strength, just as Samson did. (Samson is a biblical figure who became powerless and was enslaved after his hair was cut off by the woman he loved.)

On a Thursday afternoon, Steve is spared when Uncle Fernando (Bazelais' good friend) comes over with his barber equipment. "I don't need a haircut," Gregory complains as Fernando begins trimming the boy's hair in front of his family.

47

Steve (right) *and his cousins Stefanie* (foreground) *and Marie play in Prospect Park.*

The haircuts take place in Gregory's bedroom. In the family's small apartment, the bedroom doubles as a playroom for the children. Gregory sleeps on the top level of a bunk bed. Steve sleeps in a crib. Natalie and baby Kelly sleep in their parents' room.

Because Doudoune earns money by babysitting at home, the apartment is always filled with children. "It's fun," Gregory says. "There are kids here all the time."

In the evening, Gregory tickles Kelly and plays hide-and-seek with Steve and Natalie. The apartment is small, but there are still plenty of places to hide. The little ones either duck behind the bed or conceal themselves in the bathroom.

Several times a week, Gregory's nine-year-old cousin, Stefanie, stops by to do her homework with him. Stefanie was born in Brooklyn and speaks English as well as she speaks Creole. When Gregory's parents have trouble communicating with a neighbor or a store owner, Stefanie translates for them.

Stefanie and her family live in Gregory's building. Because Bazelais and Doudoune couldn't afford a telephone at first, their friends would call Stefanie. Then she would run out of her apartment and knock on Gregory's door. She would either deliver a message for the Beaubruns or bring Gregory's parents to the phone in her apartment.

HAITIAN PROVERBS

Short, witty sayings called proverbs are part of Haiti's rich oral tradition, which includes storytelling, riddles, word games, and songs. Many of the proverbs, which Haitians use in everyday communication, are observant, instructive, and funny. Below is a sampling of proverbs—in Creole first, followed by the English translation and an explanation in parentheses.

Creole pronunciation combines the sounds of English, Spanish, and French. Most Creole vocabulary is based on French words, although the language has borrowed from other tongues, such as Spanish, English, and various African and Caribbean languages.

Bouch manje tout manje, men li pa pale tout pawòl.
> *The mouth may eat any food but should not speak on any subject. (Discretion is important.)*

Yon sèl dwèt pa manje kalalou.
> *You can't eat okra with one finger. (We must all cooperate.)*

Chay soti sout tèt, tonbe sou zèpòl.
> *The load goes from the head to the shoulder. (Problems go from bad to worse.)*

Gras a diri, ti wòch goute grès.
> *Thanks to the rice, the pebble tastes of grease. (Good things rub off.)*

Bon kòk chante nan tout poulaye.
> *A good rooster sings to all his chickens. (A good person is sought after by everyone.)*

Byen pre pa lakay.
> *Being close by doesn't mean you're home. (Being close to wealth doesn't make you rich.)*

The above proverbs were taken from The Haitians: Their History and Culture, *a fact sheet by Michele Burtoff Civan, The Refugee Service Center, Washington, D.C., 1994.*

Gregory and Bazelais enjoy the walk to school together in the morning.

Bazelais walks Gregory to school every day. The two sometimes hold hands. They pass apartment buildings, stores, and small, brick homes. After about ten minutes, they reach P.S. 6—a modern school building with green trim. Bazelais usually takes Gregory all the way up to the front door and then takes the subway to work.

When Gregory arrived in Brooklyn, he entered first grade at P.S. 6. It was there that he learned to read and speak English. Gregory thinks that school in the United States is probably easier than in Haiti. In Haiti's tropical climate, the classrooms are always hot. And the teachers are strict. Some even hit the kids when they misbehave or get an answer wrong.

About 25 percent of the students in Gregory's school have Haitian parents. The families of most of the other youngsters are also from the West Indies. But these children come from countries where English is the main language. Because the Haitian kids don't speak English, they are often teased. Some African American kids at Gregory's school joke that the Haitians look foreign—their clothes are often old, their fashion styles out of date.

Because the weather is warm year-round in Haiti, the youngsters and their families don't come to New York with winter clothes. When they wear summer clothes to school in January or February, the other kids laugh at them. Some immigrant families can only afford one or two school outfits for each child. The kids may wear the same clothes two or three days in a row. This also leads to teasing. Some Haitian students wish that everyone wore uniforms—just like in Haiti. Then nobody would heckle them about their clothes. Fortunately Gregory has always been treated nicely by his classmates.

When Gregory is in the lunchroom or gym, he speaks English—even if he's talking to other Haitian kids. "Everybody speaks English in New York," he explains. "So I speak it, too."

In his classroom, though, lessons are taught in both English and Creole. Gregory's teacher, Mark Joseph, was born in Haiti. He is the son of a sugarcane farmer and understands how tough it is for his 20 Haitian students. "Sometimes you can speak English very well," he observes. "But Americans still can't understand your accent."

Three hours a week, Gregory and several classmates go to a separate room for English as a Second Language (ESL) class. In the ESL classes, the students improve the English they've learned since arriving in the United States.

In Gregory's regular classroom, Mr. Joseph has put up charts and posters. On one wall, the class rules are listed. All of the students in Mr. Joseph's class promise

In the United States, Gregory takes classes to improve his English. He and his teacher Ms. Cooper work on vocabulary words, such as the names of fruits and vegetables.

Gregory and his teacher Mr. Joseph work on math problems (top). *Math is Gregory's favorite subject. In the classroom, Mr. Joseph displays the Haitian flag* (above, at center) *and other items from Haiti.*

to respect each other, keep their hands to themselves, raise their hands before they speak, and do their work quietly. Important years in both U.S. and Haitian history are also posted—1941 (the year the United States entered World War II), 1963 (the year U.S. President John F. Kennedy was assassinated), and 1990 (the year Jean-Bertrand Aristide was elected president of Haiti).

Gregory likes history and is especially interested in learning about American Indians. He sees similarities to the history of his own ancestors. "It's a very sad story," he says. "The Indians were living here, and people from another country came. They kicked them off their land and killed them. It's just like the slaves who were taken from their homes in Africa."

Gregory's favorite subject is math. "A lot of people say it's hard," he says. "But math is easy for me to understand. I like learning about numbers. It's fun."

 By 1993 the United States and the United Nations (UN), an international organization, had pressured Haiti's military leader, Lieutenant General Raoul Cédras, to agree to step down and to allow Aristide to return to Haiti as president. But at the last minute, Cédras changed his mind. The United States and the UN then imposed harsh restrictions on trade and travel to Haiti. Because Cédras would not back down, the United States then prepared to invade the island. Facing an invasion, Cédras finally agreed to leave the country in October 1994, and Aristide returned to power.

UN forces, including troops from the United States, entered Haiti to keep order as Haitians began the process of switching from a government ruled by military dictators to a democracy. After an election in December 1995 and with the support of Aristide, René Préval became president of Haiti in February 1996. Préval promised to make Haiti into a strong democracy.

Gregory's family plans to stay in Brooklyn, at least for a while. Bazelais says that things may seem good in Haiti for the moment. But he's never sure if another dictator will suddenly seize power.

In the future, both Bazelais and Doudoune would like to return to the place of their birth. They miss relatives and friends still in Haiti and want to help rebuild the nation. At the same time, they've grown to appreciate the United States. "People treat you fairly here," Bazelais says. "If they see that you're a hard worker and a good family man, they respect you."

Gregory plans to study hard and to go to medical school one day. Once he becomes a doctor, he says, he'll move back to Haiti. There he'll run in the sun, swim in the ocean, and help the people he left behind.

While the Beaubruns are making the best of their new home, they hope to return to Haiti one day.

FURTHER READING

Anthony, Susan. *Haiti*. New York: Chelsea House Publishers, 1989.

Cheong-Lum, Rosaline Ng. *Haiti*. New York: Marshall Cavendish, 1995.

Goldish, Meish. *Crisis in Haiti*. Brookfield, Connecticut: The Millbrook Press, 1995.

Haiti in Pictures. Minneapolis: Lerner Publications Company, 1995.

Myers, Walter Dean. *Toussaint L'Ouverture: The Fight for Haiti's Freedom*. New York: Simon & Schuster Books for Young Readers, 1996.

Santrey, Laurence. *Toussaint L'Ouverture, Lover of Liberty*. Mahwah, New Jersey: Troll Communications, 1993.

Temple, Frances. *Taste of Salt: A Story of Modern Haiti*. New York: Orchard Books, 1992.

Wolkstein, Diane, ed. *The Magic Orange Tree and Other Haitian Folktales*. New York: Schocken Books, 1987.

PRONUNCIATION GUIDE

Aristide, Jean-Bertrand (ahr-ees-TEED, zhah[n]-behr-TRAH[n])
Beaubrun, Bazelais (boh-BRUH[n], bah-zuh-LAY)
Cédras, Raoul (say-DRAHS, rah-OOL)
Creole (KREE-ohl)
Dessalines, Jean-Jacques (day-suh-LEEN, zhah[n]-ZHAHK)
Doudoune (doo-DOON)
Duvalier, François/Jean-Claude (doo-vahl-YAY, frah[n]-SWAH/ zhah[n]-KLOHD)
Gédé (geh-DAY)
Gonâve (goh-NAHV)
Grande Cayemite (GRAH[n]D kah-yeh-MEET)
Guantánamo (gwahn-TAH-nuh-moh)
Haiti (HAY-tee)
Hispaniola (hihs-puh-NYOH-luh)
Mardi Gras (MAHR-dee grah)
Port-au-Prince (pohrt-oh-PRINS)
Préval, René (pray-VAHL, ruh-NAY)
Tontons Macoutes (toh[n]-toh[n] mah-KOOT)
Toussaint Louverture (too-SA[n] loo-vehr-TOOR)

INDEX

ABOUT THE AUTHOR

Keith Elliot Greenberg is a freelance journalist, author, and television producer specializing in real-life stories. His television credits include scripts for *America's Most Wanted, Real Life, Day and Date, Against the Law,* and *In Search of Peace,* a documentary chronicling the history of the United States in the United Nations. Mr. Greenberg has written dozens of nonfiction children's books on topics ranging from entertainment to homelessness to international terrorism. Other Lerner titles by Keith Elliot Greenberg include *An Armenian Family, Out of the Gang, Runaways,* and *Zack's Story.* A native New Yorker, Mr. Greenberg resides in Brooklyn.

PHOTO ACKNOWLEDGMENTS

Cover photographs Carol Halebian (both). All inside photos by Carol Halebian except the following: © Marc French/Panos, pp. 7, 34; © Bill Gentile/Zuma, pp. 12, 37; © Kay Shaw, pp. 17 (top), 19 (left); Archive Photos, p. 20; James Ford Bell Library, University of Minnesota, p. 21; Bettmann, p. 22; UPI/Corbis-Bettmann, p. 24; courtesy of Kaufman and Maraffi, p. 25; AFP/Corbis-Bettmann, p. 32; detail from a painting by Elie Nozier/photo by Carol Halebian, p. 36; Patrick Hamilton/Reuters/Archive Photos, p. 40; courtesy of the Port Authority of New York and New Jersey, p. 41. Wall painting cut-ins by Carol Halebian. All artwork and maps by Laura Westlund.